D0579623

Gloria J. McEwen Burgess

Pass It On!

Illustrated by Gerald Purnell

Two Sylvias Press

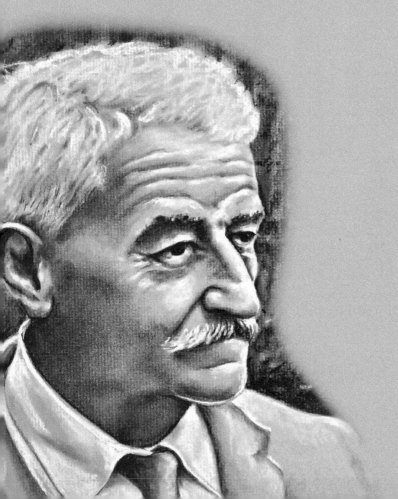

Two Sylvias Press
PO Box 1524
Kingston, WA 98346
www.twosylviaspress.com

Created with the belief that great writing is good for the world,
Two Sylvias Press mixes modern technology, classic style, and literary
intellect with an eco-friendly heart. We draw our inspiration from the
poetic literary talent of Sylvia Plath and the editorial business sense
of Sylvia Beach. We are an independent press dedicated to publishing
the exceptional voices of writers. For more information
about Two Sylvias Press, please visit: www.twosylviaspress.com.

Book Design: Breanna Powell
Cover Art: Gerald Purnell
Author Photo: John E. Burgess
Illustrator Photo: Barry S. Pugh

First Edition 2018
Created in the United States of America
ISBN: 978-0-9986314-2-4

Myra & Jane —
Thank you for
Passing it on.
Book- It ✗

Friend, McEwen Burgus

With love and gratitude
to my parents—Earnest McEwen, Jr.
and Mildred Blackmon McEwen—for your faith,
vision, perseverance, and servant hearts,
and to William Faulkner, benefactor, friend,
and kindred spirit.

And to young people everywhere,
especially those growing up without a mom or dad,
know that you are loved and blessed. Remember
to dream big, to dream out loud, to share your blessings
with others... and always remember to *pass it on!*

—G. J. M.B.

To my two granddaughters,
Tina Kamura Purnell and Olivia Katsu Klein.

—G.P.

Ernie **LOVEd** to read.

He loved to read big books, little books, long books, and short books.

His parents were too poor to buy books, but that didn't stop Ernie.

He borrowed them from his teachers, and when he found one in the trash, he'd fish it out and read it.

Ernie's family lived in a small, segregated town
called Oxford, Mississippi. To provide for their four children,
his parents had to work from sunup until sundown,
most often in the cotton fields.

They planted cotton seed in the early spring and picked
the crop all through the fall. During the picking season,
Ernie's parents worked day after day, filling their long burlap
bags with the fluffy white balls of cotton.

When the bags were full, they dragged them
to the edge of the field where the cotton was weighed
and loaded into large wooden wagons. Then the seeds
were removed, and the cotton was pressed into big bales
to be shipped down the Mississippi River.

Ernie wished his parents didn't have to work so long
and so hard. He was always glad when weekends arrived.
Every Saturday morning, the family rode to town in their
horse- or mule-drawn wagon to buy food and supplies.

In town, Ernie sometimes saw and heard things
he didn't understand, and he would get a funny feeling
inside. "Momma, why can't I use that drinking fountain?
The one we have to use says 'colored,' but the water
sure looks the same to me."

"Papa, why do we always have to go in the back door
of the grocery store? And why does Mr. Henderson
always call you 'Boy?' That's not your name,
and you're sure not a boy!"

Ernie's dad would shake his head and say,
"Hush, son. That's just the way things is."

As usual, on the long ride home, Ernie's nose was buried in a book.
He was reading one of his favorites—a book about buildings
and how they were put together.

"Someday, I'll build my very own house," he told his mother.

"You and Papa can come live with me!
We'll even have running water."

His mother just looked at him with tired, loving eyes and said, "Oh, Junior, you're such a dreamer."

"You'll see, Momma! Someday I'll even go to college! You'll see!"

But how?

Even as a young boy, Ernie knew that very few Blacks were able to go to school, let alone college. He also knew that going to college would cost a lot of money.

Every day after school, he went from house to house selling packets of seeds, using all the money he earned to buy books. His friends would follow along, teasing him for working so hard. But that never stopped Ernie.

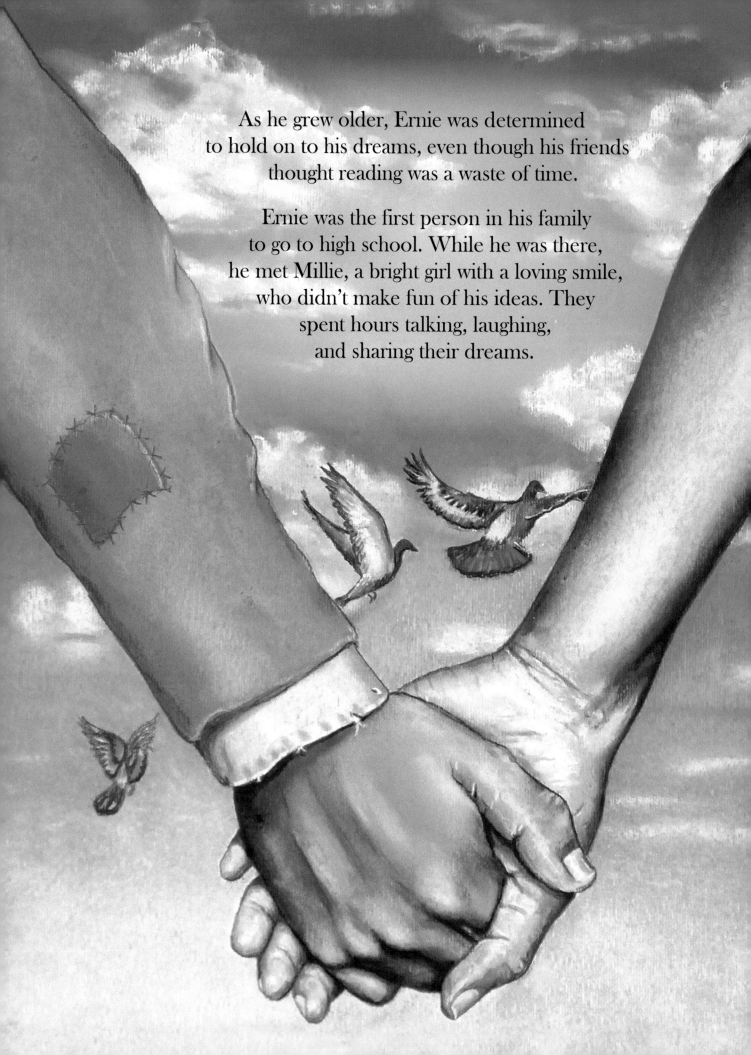

As he grew older, Ernie was determined
to hold on to his dreams, even though his friends
thought reading was a waste of time.

Ernie was the first person in his family
to go to high school. While he was there,
he met Millie, a bright girl with a loving smile,
who didn't make fun of his ideas. They
spent hours talking, laughing,
and sharing their dreams.

As time passed, they fell deeply in love
and decided to marry. When the young couple
had their first child, a precious little girl,
they named her Doris Ann.

Before long, they were blessed with two more
beautiful little girls, Annie Ruth and Gloria Jean.

Even though Ernie now had a family to support,
he still held on to his dream of going to college.
One Saturday morning he was in town sharing news
with friends, when one of his buddies called out,
"Hey, Ernie... did you hear they're lookin' for someone
to take care of those big, fancy buildings at the university?"

"Ol' Miss? I'd give anything to have a job there!"

Ernie knew that work at the university was steady, and the pay
was better than most places. It was just the kind of job he needed

Ernie woke up bright and early on Monday morning. He put on his best shirt and pants, laced up his black leather shoes, then walked through town to Ol' Miss.

A janitor's position was open—and he was hired right on the spot!

Ernie took great pride in his work and believed
that whatever the task, he should always do his very best.

He polished the floors until they glowed.

He scrubbed the toilets until they were spotless
and washed the windows until they sparkled.

While working at Ol' Miss, Ernie's love for learning grew stronger than ever. He went to work early and stayed late to read newspapers, books, old magazines—anything he could find.

Several of the teachers noticed Ernie reading day after day. One morning a kind gentleman named Dr. Guess offered to let the young man use his office before and after work. Ernie was grateful to have a quiet place to read.

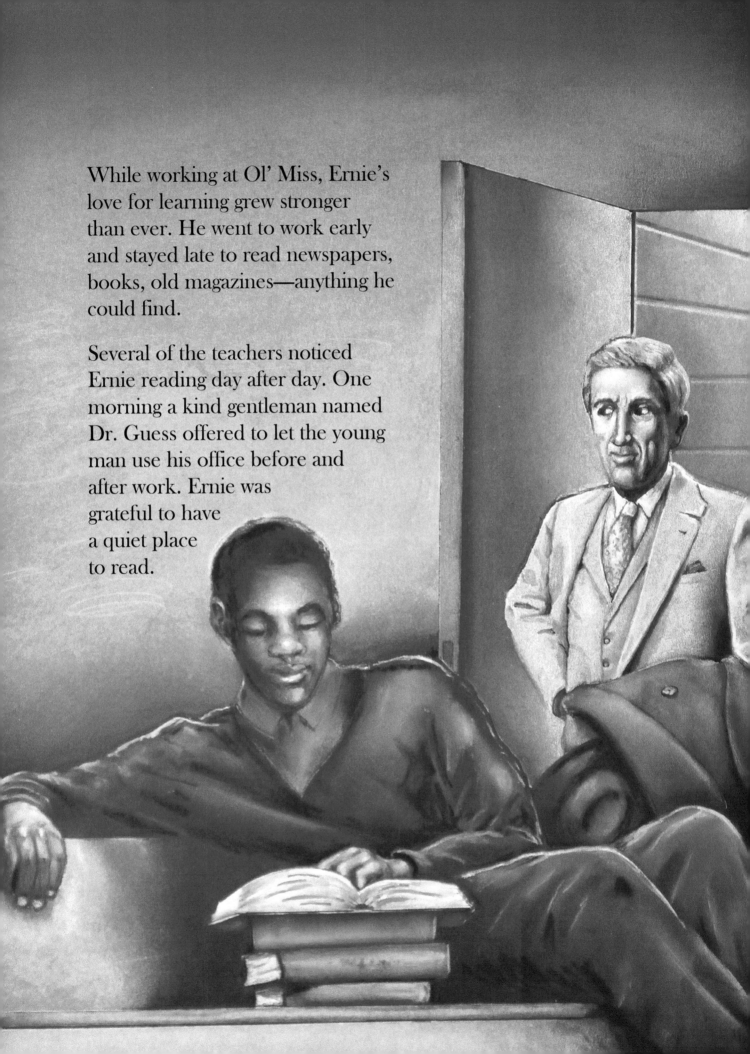

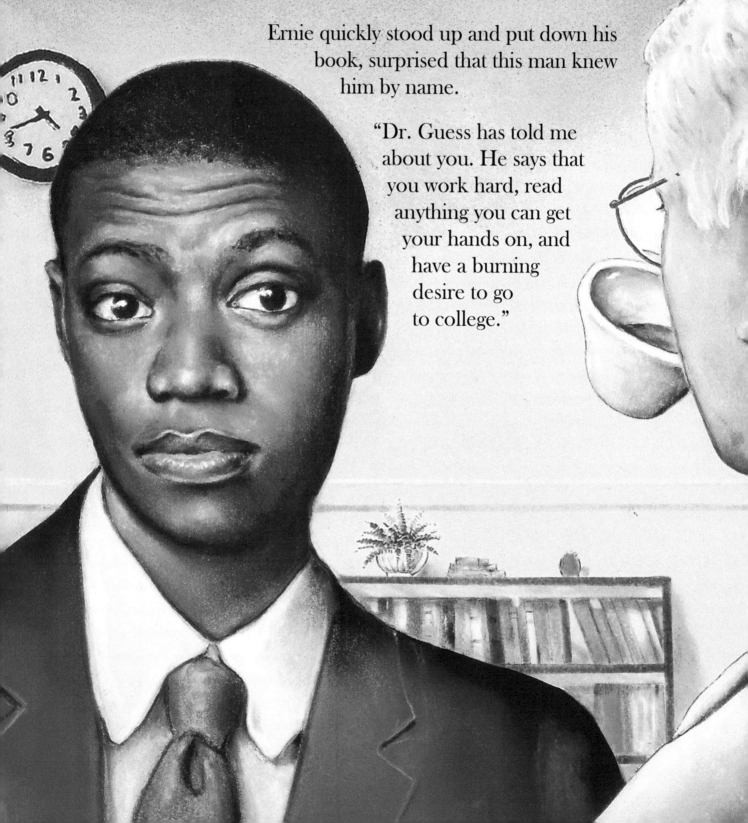

Early one morning while he was reading, Ernie heard the office door open. He looked up, expecting to see Dr. Guess. Instead, a total stranger walked in. The man wore a hat, a bow tie, and a tan-colored suit. His brown shoes were polished to a shine.

"You must be Earnest McEwen," he said.

Ernie quickly stood up and put down his book, surprised that this man knew him by name.

"Dr. Guess has told me about you. He says that you work hard, read anything you can get your hands on, and have a burning desire to go to college."

Ernie had no idea why Dr. Guess had told this stranger so much about him, but he nodded in agreement. "I love my job here at Ol' Miss, Sir, but I'd give anything to attend college myself."

"I admire your drive and determination," the man said. "My name is Dr. Love."

Dr. Love could see how deeply Ernie wanted to go to college. "Mr. McEwen," he said. "I think I know someone who might help you with your dream." He reached into his pocket and pulled out a small piece of paper with a name written on it.

"When you go to see this gentleman, tell him I sent you."

With that, Dr. Love tipped his hat and left the room.

Ernie was shocked when he read the name—William Faulkner!

He'd heard many stories about the reclusive writer
who lived at Rowan Oak, a large, old home at the edge
of town. But like most people in Oxford, Ernie had never met
the world-famous author.

Amazed and puzzled, he carefully tucked the paper
into his pocket, wondering why this man would even care

The next day, Ernie put on his Sunday-best clothes and black leather shoes. As he walked up the long stone pathway to Rowan Oak, he didn't know what to expect.

When he reached the front door, Ernie took a deep breath and knocked, then waited nervously.

A dark-skinned woman in a yellow dress and white apron opened the door, greeting him with a friendly smile. "You must be Earnest McEwen. Mr. Faulkner has been expecting you. Please wait here

As Mr. Faulkner
walked toward
him, Ernie's heart
was pounding, but
to his surprise he felt
immediately at ease
with the celebrated writer.

They talked for hours that afternoon
in the shade of the giant oak trees
surrounding the house. Mr. Faulkner
listened intently as Ernie spoke
about his lifelong dream
of going to college.

"Ever since I was a boy,
I've loved to read books.

From these books, I've learned that things
can be very different from the way they are
here in Oxford. My wife and I have struggled
all our lives, but we've never forgotten our dreams.
We want our girls to have a better life
than we've had."

Mr. Faulkner could feel Ernie's passion
for learning and saw the determination
in his eyes. "Mr. McEwen," he asked,
"do you have a college in mind?"

"Yes, Sir," Ernie said, "Alcorn. It's a long way
from here, over 200 miles. But I've heard
it's a wonderful school that provides a solid
education for Blacks."

"Excellent choice, Mr. McEwen. If I may,
I'd like to help you with your dream."

Ernie couldn't believe his ears!

At first, he was overjoyed.

But after a long silence, he slowly shook his head.
"I want to go to college more than anything in the world,
but I can't accept your generous offer. I just don't see
how I'd ever be able to pay you back."

With a twinkle in his eye, Mr. Faulkner smiled.
"I don't expect you to pay me back! I'm just glad I can help
you and your family."

"But Sir, how can I ever thank you?"

The famous author reached out to shake Ernie's hand.
"Mr. McEwen, the only thing I would ask is that when
someone else needs a kindness, you pass it on."

Before leaving Rowan Oak, Ernie stopped at the edge of the woods and knelt on the cool grass beside an old magnolia tree.

With tears flowing down his cheeks, he said a prayer of gratitude for his family, Dr. Guess, Dr. Love, and William Faulkner.

With each step on the long walk home,
Mr. Faulkner's words echoed in Ernie's mind,

"Pass it on...

Pass it on...

Pass it on."

Ernie couldn't wait to tell his family the good news. When he saw Millie standing on the front porch, he ran to her as fast as he could. "Mr. Faulkner is helping me go to Alcorn!"

Millie threw her arms around him and they danced with joy. But her mind was racing with questions.

How will we live so far apart for so long?

Will I be able to raise our daughters all by myself?

Even with her worries, Millie laughed as she watched her husband twirling around the porch with their youngest daughter, Gloria Jean. Ernie's face was glowing.

"There's more, Millie," he said with a grin. "We're all going to Alcorn—you, me, and our girls!"

Now it was Millie who couldn't believe her ears.
Ernie squeezed her hand and gathered his family around.

"We are so blessed. We have each other, we have our faith, and now our dream is finally coming true."

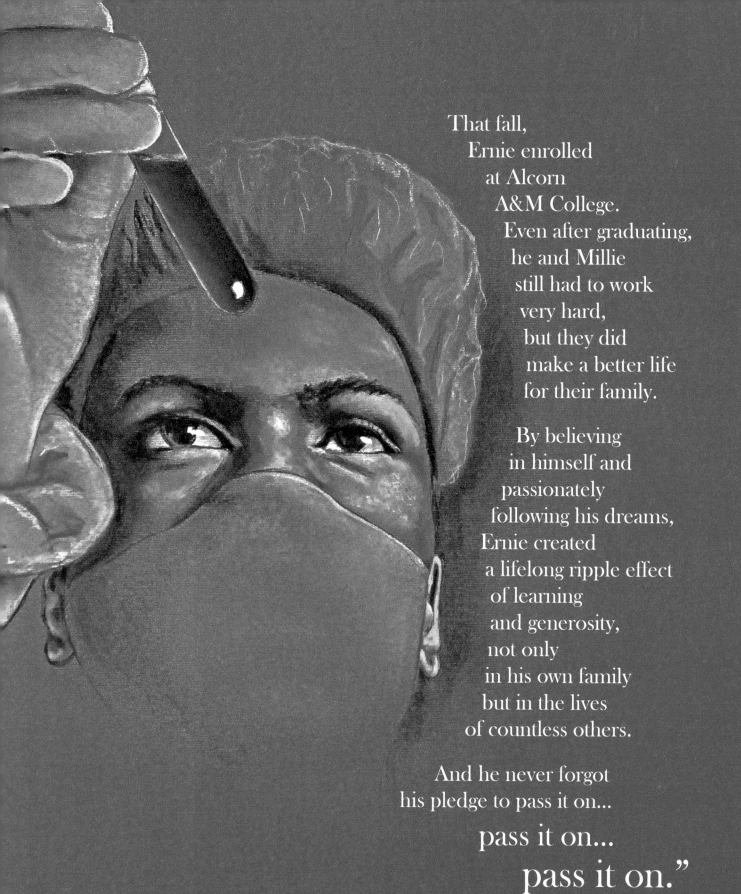

That fall,
Ernie enrolled
at Alcorn
A&M College.
Even after graduating,
he and Millie
still had to work
very hard,
but they did
make a better life
for their family.

By believing
in himself and
passionately
following his dreams,
Ernie created
a lifelong ripple effect
of learning
and generosity,
not only
in his own family
but in the lives
of countless others.

And he never forgot
his pledge to pass it on...

pass it on...

pass it on."

Author's Note

As promised, Mr. Faulkner made payments each month to Alcorn so Ernie could pursue his lifelong dream. He also arranged for Ernie and Millie to work at Alcorn, as a janitor and nursery school teacher, so the family could live together near the college.

Dr. Leston L. Love and Dr. Malcolm Guess also helped to support the family, making sure they always had food and provisions. Dr. Love sent boxes of clothes and shoes that his own daughters had outgrown. When money was short, an envelope always seemed to arrive just in time.

Ernie's love of learning led him into a career as a lab technician and later into engineering. He also accomplished his dream of living in a house with running water and even created the blueprint to build his own dream house. Before he could build it, Ernie died of an illness at the age of 56, knowing that his legacy would be carried on by his family and friends.

Ernie never forgot Mr. Faulkner, Dr. Guess, or Dr. Love. These men acted in ways that were quite extraordinary for their time, and they maintained friendships with one another throughout their lives.

Ernie and Millie passed their generosity and love of learning to each of their five daughters: Doris Ann, Annie Ruth, Gloria Jean, Deborah Anita, and Vera Antoinette.

Millie McEwen continues to reach out to children—not just her own, but to all children.

Dr. Doris McEwen, a former school superintendent, is now a university administrator who creates education reform.

Annie McEwen, a social worker and community servant, mentors youth and helps people of all ages with special learning needs.

Dr. Gloria McEwen Burgess is an inspirational speaker, leadership consultant, executive coach, civic leader, educator, poet, and author.

Dr. Deborah McEwen loves mentoring and caring for youth. A former computer engineer, she is now a pediatrician.

Vera McEwen has a heart for those who are hurting, those seeking spiritual care. A former computer engineer and cranio-sacral therapist, she is now a pastor.

Blessed by the generosity and passion for lifelong learning passed on by their parents and William Faulkner, Ernie and Millie's daughters continue to pass their blessings on to people around the world.

GRATITUDES

It takes a village to bring a book into the world.

With deep gratitude to my fellow villagers. My amazing illustrator Gerald Purnell. My editorial team—inspiring publishers Kelli Russell Agodon and Annette Spaulding-Convy of Two Sylvias Press and wonderful book designer Breanna Powell. My muses Earnest McEwen, Jr., Mildred Blackmon McEwen, and William Faulkner.

A very special thanks to Conrad Wesselhoeft and Jeanie Davies Okimoto. Outside of my family, Conrad was one of the first listeners to hear about my father's relationship with William Faulkner. Sensing that I'd never shared this with others, he urged me to write it down. "Gloria, if you don't write about your father and Faulkner, someone else will. And it will be their version of your father's life. Not yours."

When I first wrote about my father and William Faulkner, poems emerged. Then the density of dialogue and intensely vibrant images. When I realized I was writing a picture book, I called my friend Jeanie. An insightful author of books for young people, she encouraged me to let young Ernie lead the way. Following her sage advice, I learned a great deal about the visionary, determined young boy who would become my father.

Gerald and I extend our thanks to libraries everywhere, particularly the Voorhees Public Library in Echelon, New Jersey; University of Mississippi Library in Oxford, Mississippi; and Edmonds Public Library in Edmonds, Washington. We're also grateful to photographer Martin J. Dain for his book *Faulkner's County: Yoknapatawpha*. Published over 50 years ago, this volume of black and white photographs was a particularly unique and valuable resource.

My heartfelt thanks to the villagers who made this book possible—book whisperers all.

Siri Alderson • Gloria Russell-Baker • Susan Bradbury
Angela Braun-LeBaw • Katherine Grace Bond • Susannah Bruck
Anomi Bruynius • John Burgess • Skye Burn • Kelley Butler • Leanna McEwen Chandler
Toi Derricotte • Anne Depue • Kwame Dawes • Cornelius Eady • Jennifer Ford • Kelley Froedel • William Griffith
R. Malcolm Guess • Monica Harrold • Andrea Hurst • Chelsea Kern • Margy Kotick • William Lewis, Jr. • Leston L. Love
Nan Macy • Paul Martinelli • Annie McEwen • Deborah McEwen • Doris McEwen • Vera McEwen • Marilyn Nelson
Helen Nobrega • Londa Ogden • Toni O'Neal • Jesse R. Otis • Elizabeth Purnell • Sparky Reardon
Kathy Sangster • Marilyn Shoeman • Marion Smith, Jr. • Square Books
Jenn Sundt • John Thompson • Kimmie Thompson

GLORIA J. MCEWEN BURGESS is an inspirational speaker, leadership consultant, executive coach, civic leader, educator, poet, and author. She has written six books, including three books of poetry. *Pass It On!* is her first book for children. An award-winning poet, performer, and speaker, she has served as an artist-in-residence at many schools and has been a featured artist on National Public Radio (NPR) and the BBC. Gloria teaches transformational leadership at Seattle University, University of Washington, and University of Southern California. She has traveled extensively throughout North America, Africa, Europe, Australia, and South America. A lifelong champion for children, learning, and those who are impacted by institutional oppression, Dr. McEwen Burgess is Founder and Executive Director of The Lift Every Voice Foundation, a non-profit organization that provides leadership development for vulnerable youth and their teachers. Recognized by The HistoryMakers as a living legacy for her contributions and service as a leader, Gloria is also an artist-scholar for Humanities Washington and a Cave Canem Fellow, a prestigious collective of poets and writers of the African Diaspora. You can contact Gloria at gloria@gloriaburgess.com.

GERALD PURNELL'S art is exquisitely evocative, expressing his deep compassion and love for others. As a fine artist and illustrator, his arresting, colorful art celebrates diversity and the indomitable power of the human spirit, winning him acclaim and numerous awards. Gerald's artwork is featured on all 21 covers of the acclaimed Bluford Series, young-adult novels distributed by Scholastic Books. He has been interviewed on NPR and Philadelphia's WHYY radio. For his work with troubled youth, he received a letter of commendation from the city of Philadelphia. He also won the coveted Christopher Award for Outstanding Achievement for the Betterment of Mankind in the children's picture book category. His award-winning picture books include *Am I a Color Too?*, *God's Promise*, and *A Home Run for Bunny*, published by Illumination Arts. *Pass It On!* is Gerald's fourth picture book. You can contact him at g.purnell@comcast.net.